Practice MAKES PERFECT

Reading
Comprehension

Author
Teacher Created
Resources Staff

Managing Editor
Eric Migliaccio

Editor in Chief
Brent L. Fox, M. Ed.

Creative Director
Sarah M. Fournier

Cover Artist
Diem Pascarella

Art Coordinator
Renée Mc Elwee

Illustrator
Kevin Cameron

Imaging
Amanda R. Harter

Publisher
Mary D. Smith, M.S. Ed.

Teacher Created Resources
12621 Western Avenue
Garden Grove, CA 92841
www.teachercreated.com

ISBN: 978-1-4206-2078-8

©2024 Teacher Created Resources

Made in U.S.A.

For standards correlations, visit
http://www.teachercreated.com/standards/

Teacher Created Resources

Table of Contents

Introduction

The old adage "practice makes perfect" can really hold true for children and their education. The more practice child has with concepts being taught in school, the more success they are likely to find. For many parents, knowing how to achieve this goal and support their child's learning can be frustrating. This book is designed to eliminate the guesswork for parents using it at home, while also being a valuable resource for educators using it in the classroom.

Here's how: By pairing short, easy-to-understand fiction and nonfiction passages with large illustrations that depict the action of the story, this book helps prepare young learners for reading. Each passage is followed by two reading comprehension questions to ask students to ensure that they are fully understanding what they are hearing, seeing, and reading.

For Grade K, *Practice Makes Perfect: Reading Comprehension* covers the following skills:

- understanding level-appropriate sight words and vocabulary
- reading and listening to stories in a variety of genres (fiction, nonfiction, and informational)
- matching written text to illustrations
- answer basic comprehension questions (who, what, when, where, why, and how)
- find the best answer and fill in the appropriate bubble beside that answer.

Inside This Resource

Reading Passages and Comprehension Questions (pages 4–45) — There are 42 reading passages that have been divided into three categories: fiction, nonfiction, and informational. These passages can be read sequentially or can be done out of order, as needed.

Answer Sheets (page 46) — These optional sheets provide a similar format to those found on standardized tests. Use these "bubble-in" answer sheets in the classroom or at home.

Answer Key (page 47) — This key provides the answers for all of the comprehension questions that accompany the passages.

Make Your Own Story (page 48) — After reading these stories and looking at the pictures that accompany them, your child may be inspired to write and illustrate their own story. Encourage them to write on the lines provided at the bottom of this template page and draw a picture in the box at the top.

Helpful Tips

- Keep practice sessions short, positive, and constructive.
- Read the passages aloud for your child until they are ready to read them independently.
- Provide extra guidance and support in the areas in which your child is struggling. Look for ways to apply these skills to real-life situations.

Name: _____

The Cat and the Rat

The cat saw the rat. The rat ran. The cat ran after the rat.

1. What animal saw the rat?
   A. a cat
   B. a dog

2. What did the cat do?
   A. It ran after the rat.
   B. It drank some milk.

Name: _____

The Park

Pam likes to go to the park. She likes to slide fast on the big slide. She likes to go on the swings. The park is fun.

1. Who likes to go to the park?
   - (A) Polly
   - (B) Pam

2. How does she like to slide?
   - (A) fast
   - (B) slow

Name: _____

Sam's Pet Fish

Sam has a fish for a pet. He named him Jerry.
Sam feeds Jerry once a day. Sam likes his fish.

1. What is the name of the fish in the story?
   - Ⓐ Sam
   - Ⓑ Jerry

2. How many times a day is the fish fed?
   - Ⓐ one time
   - Ⓑ two times

Name: _____

The Hike

Tim and his dad went on a long hike. They went up a big hill. They ate lunch. It was a great day!

⋯⋯⋯⋯⋯⋯⋯⋯⋯⋯⋯⋯⋯⋯⋯⋯⋯⋯⋯⋯⋯⋯⋯⋯⋯⋯⋯⋯⋯⋯⋯⋯⋯⋯⋯⋯⋯⋯

1. Where did Tim and his dad go?
   - Ⓐ   on a hike
   - Ⓑ   to a baseball game

2. What did they eat?
   - Ⓐ   dinner
   - Ⓑ   lunch

Name: _____

The Chick

The yellow chick sleeps in the barn. She eats in the sun. She says, "Peep, peep," all day long.

....

1. What animal sleeps in the barn?
   - (A) a sheep
   - (B) a yellow chick

2. What sounds does the animal make?
   - (A) "Peep, peep."
   - (B) "Baa, baa."

Name: _____

Helping

Jake likes to help. He helps his mom wash the dishes. He helps his dad wash the car. He is a good helper.

I. Who does Jake help wash the dishes?

Ⓐ   his mom

Ⓑ   his dad

2. What does Jake help his dad wash?

Ⓐ   the car

Ⓑ   the dishes

Name: _____

The Ice Cream Truck

It was a very hot day. Luke wanted some ice cream. He heard the ice cream truck coming. What a treat!

I. What did Luke want?

Ⓐ   some cookies

Ⓑ   some ice cream

2. What did he hear coming?

Ⓐ   the ice cream truck

Ⓑ   a fire truck

Name: _____

The Kite

Jack has a kite. It is blue and yellow. It goes up high in the sky. Jack likes flying his kite.

1. What does Jack have?
   - Ⓐ an airplane
   - Ⓑ a kite

2. What color is it?
   - Ⓐ green and purple
   - Ⓑ blue and yellow

Name: _____

The Picnic

Milly and Billy went to a park. They packed good food to eat. They found a sunny place to sit. They put the food on a blanket. Watch out for ants!

1. Where did Milly and Billy go?
   - (A) to a park
   - (B) to a beach

2. What did they pack?
   - (A) toys
   - (B) food

Name: _____

The Race

Jane and Jill wanted to race. Ready, set, go! Off ran Jane. Off ran Jill. Jane ran faster. She won the race.

1. Who wanted to race?
   - (A) Jen and Jim
   - (B) Jane and Jill

2. Who ran faster?
   - (A) Jane
   - (B) Jill

Name: _____

The Sail Boat

There is a boat out on the lake. It is sailing in the wind. It is rocking on the waves. What fun!

I. What is out on the lake?

Ⓐ a boat

Ⓑ a duck

2. What is it rocking on?

Ⓐ the sails

Ⓑ the waves

Name: _____

The Frog

There was once a big green frog. He lived in a pond. He liked to eat bugs. He liked to hop. He liked to sit in the sun.

1. Where did the frog live?
   - Ⓐ   a lake
   - Ⓑ   a pond

2. What did he like to eat?
   - Ⓐ   bugs
   - Ⓑ   fish

Name: _____

Soccer

Pete plays soccer in the summer. He likes kicking the ball. He likes playing with friends. The best part is when he makes a goal.

I. Who likes to play soccer?

Ⓐ Pete

Ⓑ Summer

2. What is the best part?

Ⓐ when he runs

Ⓑ when he makes a goal

Name: _____

The Old Fat Cat

There is an old fat cat. He lives in a big red barn. The cat likes to sleep in the sweet soft hay.

1. Where does the old fat cat live?
   - Ⓐ in a big yellow house
   - Ⓑ in a big red barn

2. Where does the cat like to sleep?
   - Ⓐ on an old soft rug
   - Ⓑ in the sweet soft hay

Name: _____

Snow

Snow is wet. Snow is cold. Snow can be fun.

1. What word tells us about snow?

Ⓐ wet

Ⓑ dry

2. How does snow feel?

Ⓐ warm

Ⓑ cold

Name: _____

The Beach

The beach is hot. The beach has sand. The beach has waves.

....

1. How does the beach feel?

Ⓐ   hot

Ⓑ   cold

2. What does the beach have?

Ⓐ   mud

Ⓑ   sand

Name: _____

On the Farm

There are animals on the farm. There are cows.
There are horses. There are pigs.

1. What animals are on the farm?
   - (A) tigers
   - (B) cows

2. What other animals are on the farm?
   - (A) pigs
   - (B) monkeys

Name: _____

In Spring

In the spring, birds sing. Bees buzz. Rain falls.
Flowers grow.

1. What sings in the spring?
    (A) trees
    (B) birds

2. What grows in the spring?
    (A) flowers
    (B) houses

Name: _____

At School

We read books at school. We write stories. We play with our friends.

I. What do we do at school?

   Ⓐ   take dogs on walks

   Ⓑ   read books

2. What else do we do at school?

   Ⓐ   play with our family

   Ⓑ   play with our friends

Name: _____

A Spider's Web

A spider's web is made of silk. The silk is sticky. Spiders use their webs to catch food.

I. What is a spider's web made of?

    (A)   glue

    (B)   silk

2. What do spiders use their webs to do?

    (A)   make silk

    (B)   catch food

Name: _____

Ice Cream

Ice cream is cold. You eat it on a cone or in a bowl.
Ice cream melts.

....

1. How does ice cream feel?

Ⓐ   cold

Ⓑ   hot

2. How do you eat ice cream?

Ⓐ   on a cone

Ⓑ   in a shoe

Name: _____

The Sun

The sun is hot. The sun gives light. The sun helps plants grow.

I. How does the sun feel?

(A)   light

(B)   hot

2. What does the sun do?

(A)   help plants grow

(B)   help houses grow

Name: _____

Birds

Birds can fly. Birds build nests and lay eggs.
Birds eat worms.

1. What do birds eat?
   - (A) worms
   - (B) snakes

2. What can birds do?
   - (A) fly
   - (B) run backwards

Name: _____

Our Home

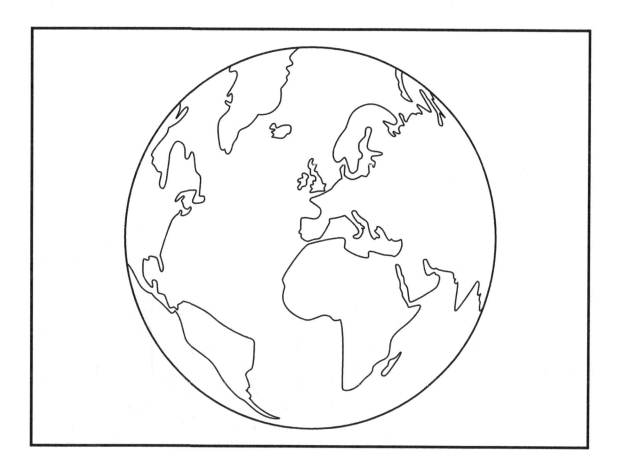

Earth is a planet. It has lots of land. It has even more water than land. Earth is our home.

I. What is Earth?

Ⓐ   a plant

Ⓑ   a planet

2. What does Earth have more of?

Ⓐ   water

Ⓑ   land

Name: _____

Cows

Cows give milk. Cows eat grass. Cows say "moo."

1. What do cows give us?

Ⓐ juice

Ⓑ milk

2. What do cows eat?

Ⓐ grass

Ⓑ cheese

Name: _____

In Fall

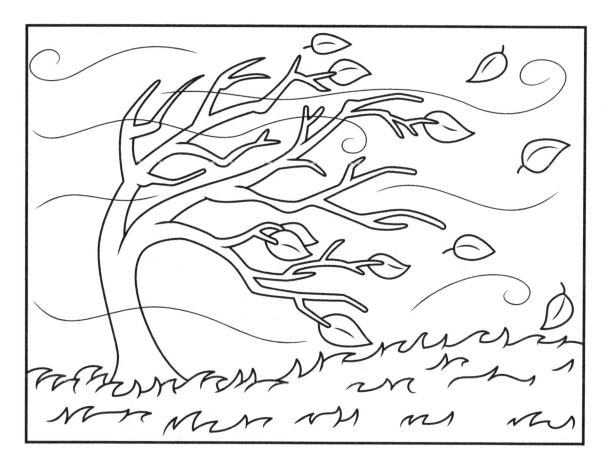

In the fall, the wind blows. The leaves fall. The days get colder. Winter is coming.

1. What happens in the fall?

   Ⓐ   The flowers bloom.

   Ⓑ   The leaves fall.

2. What comes after the fall?

   Ⓐ   the winter

   Ⓑ   the summer

Name: _____

Grapes

Grapes grow on vines. They are green, red, or purple.
Grapes are juicy and round.

I. Where do grapes grow?

Ⓐ   on vines

Ⓑ   on trees

2. What colors are grapes?

Ⓐ   green, red, and purple

Ⓑ   blue, pink, and yellow

Name: _____

Frost

There is frost on the grass. There is frost on the car. Frost comes when it is cold.

1. Where is the frost?
   - (A) on the grass
   - (B) in the house

2. When does it come?
   - (A) when it is hot
   - (B) when it is cold

Name: _____

Using a Library Book

- Wash your hands.

- Keep the book safe from pets and babies.

- Bring the book back on time.

....

1. What do you need to keep your library books safe from?

   (A)   pets and babies

   (B)   moms and dads

2. When do you bring the book back to the library?

   (A)   late

   (B)   on time

Name: _____

In My Pencil Box

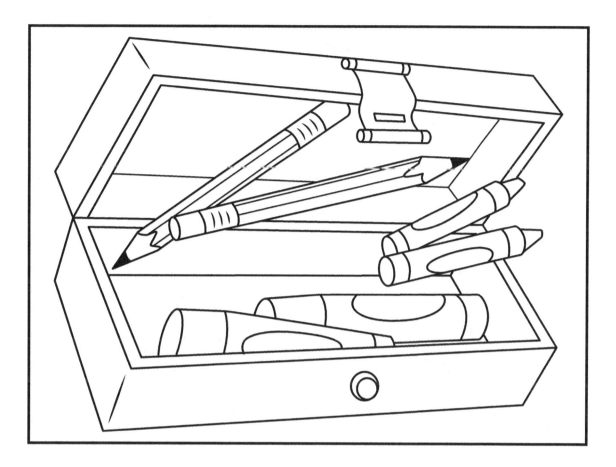

- There are crayons in my pencil box.

- There are pencils in my pencil box.

- There are markers in my pencil box.

1. What is in the pencil box?

   Ⓐ   food

   Ⓑ   crayons

2. Where are the markers?

   Ⓐ   in the pencil box

   Ⓑ   in the backpack

Name: _____

Making S'Mores

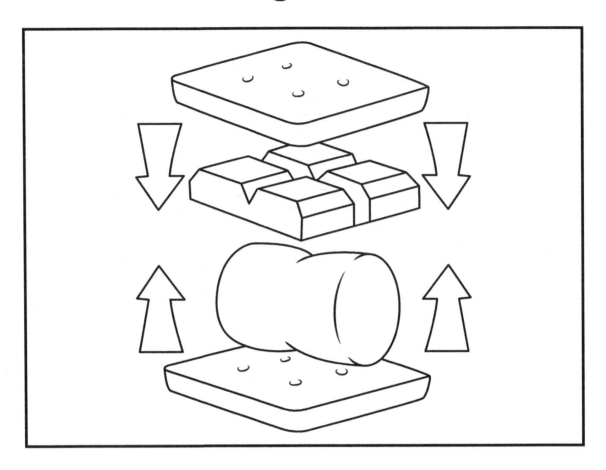

- Get two sweet graham crackers.

- Put chocolate and marshmallow in the middle.

- Eat the treat. Yum!

1. What kind of cracker should you use?
   - (A) salty
   - (B) sweet

2. What goes in the middle?
   - (A) chocolate and marshmallow
   - (B) ham and cheese

Name: _____

Making Pizza

Step 1: Roll out the dough.

Step 2: Spread sauce on the dough.

Step 3: Put cheese on top.

Step 4: Bake the pizza in the oven.

1. What is the first step to make a pizza?

Ⓐ   Roll out the dough.

Ⓑ   Bake it in the oven.

2. What is the last step to make a pizza?

Ⓐ   Put cheese on top.

Ⓑ   Bake it in the oven.

Name: _____

Bus Rules

- Sit in your seat on the bus.

- No yelling on the bus.

- Don't stick any part of yourself out of the window.

I. What should you do on the bus?

Ⓐ   Stand up.

Ⓑ   Sit in your seat.

2. What should you **not** do on the bus?

Ⓐ   Talk quietly.

Ⓑ   Yell.

Name: _____

Getting Ready for School

- Get dressed.

- Eat healthy food.

- Brush your teeth.

....

I. What do you need to do to get ready for school?

   (A)   Play outside.

   (B)   Get dressed.

2. What else do you need to do to get ready for school?

   (A)   Eat good food.

   (B)   Eat candy.

Name: _____

Lily's Lunch Box

- Lily has a sandwich in her lunch box.

- Lily has a drink in her lunch box.

- Lily has an apple in her lunch box.

1. What is in Lily's lunch box?
   Ⓐ   a sandwich
   Ⓑ   a book

2. What else is in Lily's lunch box?
   Ⓐ   an apple
   Ⓑ   a banana

Name: _____

Planting Seeds

Step 1: Dig a hole.

Step 2: Put seeds in the hole.

Step 3: Cover the seeds with dirt.

Step 4: Water the seeds.

Step 5: Wait for them to grow.

1. What do you do first to plant seeds?

   Ⓐ   Dig a hole.

   Ⓑ   Wait for it to grow.

2. What do you do last when you plant seeds?

   Ⓐ   Dig a hole.

   Ⓑ   Wait for them to grow.

Name: _____

Zoo Rules

- Do not feed the animals.

- Do not put your hands in their cages.

- Throw all of your trash in the garbage can.

- Stay with your group.

1. What should you **not** do at the zoo?
   - Ⓐ   Look at the animals.
   - Ⓑ   Feed the animals.

2. What should you do at the zoo?
   - Ⓐ   Stay with your group.
   - Ⓑ   Leave your group to look at animals.

Name: _____

Taking Care of a Fish

- Give him fish food.

- Keep him wet.

- Clean his tank.

....

1. How do you take care of a fish?
   - (A)   Give him fish food.
   - (B)   Give him gum.

2. What is another way to take care of a fish?
   - (A)   Keep him wet.
   - (B)   Keep him dry.

Name: _____

Cleaning Your Room

- Put your dirty clothes in the hamper.

- Pick up the toys.

- Put the books on the shelf.

- Now you have room to play!

1. Where do you put the dirty clothes?
   - Ⓐ in the hamper
   - Ⓑ on the floor

2. Where do you put your books?
   - Ⓐ on the bed
   - Ⓑ on the shelf

Name: _____

Snowball Fight

- Pick up a big handful of snow.

- Pack it really tight to make it into a ball.

- Throw it at a friend.

1. What do you have to pick up to have a snowball fight?

    Ⓐ   a small handful of mud

    Ⓑ   a big handful of snow

2. What do you do with it?

    Ⓐ   Keep it in your hand.

    Ⓑ   Throw it at a friend.

Name: _____

Show and Tell

Step 1: Bring a toy to school.

Step 2: Let the class see it.

Step 3: Tell the class about it.

1. What is the first step to doing a show and tell?

   Ⓐ   Bring a toy to school.

   Ⓑ   Tell the class about it.

2. What is the last step to doing a show and tell?

   Ⓐ   Bring a toy to school.

   Ⓑ   Tell the class about it.

Name: _____

At a Birthday Party

- Have friends come to your house.
- Play games, eat cake, and open presents.
- Have fun!

....

1. What do you eat at a birthday party?

(A) cake

(B) presents

2. What do you do at a birthday party?

(A) read books

(B) open presents

Name: _____

Answer Sheets

Reading Passage

_____

_____

Title

1. Ⓐ Ⓑ

2. Ⓐ Ⓑ

Reading Passage

_____

_____

Title

1. Ⓐ Ⓑ

2. Ⓐ Ⓑ

Reading Passage

_____

_____

Title

1. Ⓐ Ⓑ

2. Ⓐ Ⓑ

Reading Passage

_____

_____

Title

1. Ⓐ Ⓑ

2. Ⓐ Ⓑ

Answer Key

page 4
1. A
2. A

page 5
1. B
2. A

page 6
1. B
2. A

page 7
1. A
2. B

page 8
1. B
2. A

page 9
1. A
2. A

page 10
1. B
2. A

page 11
1. B
2. B

page 12
1. A
2. B

page 13
1. B
2. A

page 14
1. A
2. B

page 15
1. B
2. A

page 16
1. A
2. B

page 17
1. B
2. B

page 18
1. A
2. B

page 19
1. A
2. B

page 20
1. B
2. A

page 21
1. B
2. A

page 22
1. B
2. B

page 23
1. B
2. B

page 24
1. A
2. A

page 25
1. B
2. A

page 26
1. A
2. A

page 27
1. B
2. A

page 28
1. B
2. A

page 29
1. B
2. A

page 30
1. A
2. A

page 31
1. A
2. B

page 32
1. A
2. B

page 33
1. B
2. A

page 34
1. B
2. A

page 35
1. A
2. B

page 36
1. B
2. B

page 37
1. B
2. A

page 38
1. A
2. A

page 39
1. A
2. B

page 40
1. B
2. A

page 41
1. A
2. A

page 42
1. A
2. B

page 43
1. B
2. B

page 44
1. A
2. B

page 45
1. A
2. B

Name: _____

Make Your Own Story

_____

_____

_____

_____

_____

_____

_____

_____

_____

_____

_____

Made in the USA
Middletown, DE
06 September 2024

60484291R00031